ARI LEWIS

BOOK

ABOUT THE AUTHOR

Twenty-four-year-old Shari Lewis was groomed from infancy for the stardom she now enjoys. Her mother is a music teacher, and her father, Dr. Abraham B. Hurwitz—now director of student activities at Yeshiva University—is himself a skilled magician and showman. He began instructing Shari in the ways of magic and other theatrical arts before she was two. At the age of four, she appeared on stage with him, and her show business career was launched.

Later, Shari attended Manhattan's High School of Music & Art, the American School of Ballet, the Neighborhood Playhouse and Columbia University. Sandwiched in were USO shows with her father and appearances on the strawhat circuit.

Shari's main ambition was to be a dancer. A broken leg put an end to that dream. But it turned out to be the luckiest break she could have had, for while she was recuperating, her father bought her a puppet and she began to experiment with ventriloquism to pass the idle hours. Three months later, she was a winner on Arthur Godfrey's Talent Scouts.

Less than a year after that—at the age of 18—Shari developed her own TV show, "Facts 'n Fun." A series of other programs followed, culminating in 1957 in "Shariland" and "Hi Mom." Since then her rise has been meteoric and well documented. Her most recent foray has been into the recording field with "Fun in Shariland," an immediate best seller.

Recently married to TV producer Jeremy Tarcher, Shari looks forward to combining her whirlwind career in show business with that of wife and mother—say, "about three children . . . "

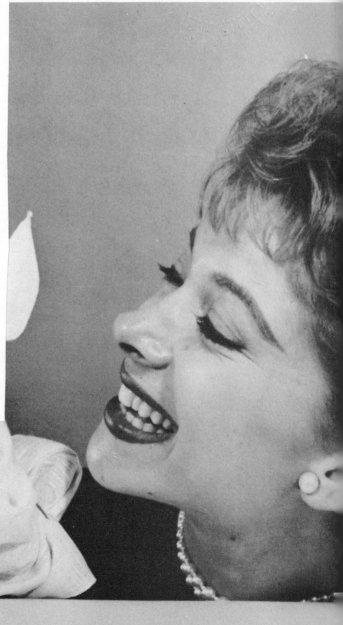

WITH PHOTOGRAPHS BY

Arthur Leipzig

AND DRAWINGS BY

Larry Lurin

DEDICATION

To the men in my life:

My Dad, who urged me to start this book . . .
My husband, who encouraged me to finish it . . .
My publisher, who insisted . . .

CONTENTS

The Puppets

The Scissor Bird 6
Fly-by-Night, the Envelope
  Bird 7
Hanky Panky 8
*Hand*some Johnny 10
Your Gum-Chum 11
Thumbelina 12
Chicky Mickey 14
Apple Jack 'n Jill 16
Ella Fant, the Pachyderm
  Puppet 18
Winky 20
Octopussy Cat 21

Captain Carrot 24
Willy B. Brave, the Matchbox
  Indian 26
The Funny Bunny 28
Bouncer, the Ball Clown 30
Coppelia, the Dancing Hand-
  kerchief 32
Sad Sack, the Bunny 34
Santa's the Name (But He's Just
  a Shell of His Former Self) 36
Boo Hoo, the Little Ghost 38
Terry, the Washcloth Pussycat 40
Hippity Hop 43

Witch Hazel 44

Basic Directions

Whiskers 47
Drape Puppet Body 48

Drape-Around-Stick Body 50
Catstairs 51

Glove Body 52

Puppet Stages

Apron Stage 53
Cardboard Carton Stage 54

Puppet Tray Stage 55
Doorway Stage 56

101 Ways to Have Fun with Puppets

Some of My Best Friends Are
  Puppets 57
Rainy-Day Box 58

Fiddle the Riddle 59
Storytime 60
Sing Along 61

The Scissor Bird

These scissor birds are so easy, I'll bet you can figure them out without any help. For these puppets you will need:

- *A sheet of construction paper (or other stiff paper)*
- *Crayons*
- *A blunt pair of scissors*

Here's how:

Draw a silly-looking bird, front or side view. Perhaps you'd like to add a real feather tail as I have. Next, draw two funny eyes, but instead of drawing the beak, stick the blades of a blunt pair of scissors through the paper at the spot where the beak should be. Now you can open or close your bird's beak by opening and closing the pair of scissors from behind the paper (which will cover your hand). If your bird becomes hungry, feed him scraps of paper and watch him chew them to pieces. Isn't he a cute cut-up?

Just for fun, try making the same bird with a pair of pliers instead of scissors. Your bird will become a hook-beaked parrot.

Why not make a pair of these scissor bird-brains. After all—two heads are better than one!

Fly-by-Night, the Envelope Bird

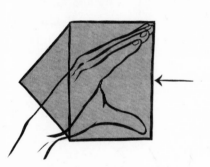

This talking bird is really worth writing home about. For this bird you will need:
  - *An envelope*

Here's how:

Place your hand, either one, into an envelope, with your fingers tucked into the corners, as in the first picture. At the arrow, press in with the fingers of the other hand. Now as you open and close your hand inside the envelope, your bird will open and close his beak. Complete your bird by adding an eye (in crayon, ink, or perhaps a postage stamp), and your talking envelope bird is sure to win the stamp of approval of all your friends.

Hanky Panky

Any magician can pull a rabbit out of a hat, but can you pull a rabbit out of a handkerchief? It's easy. For this puppet you will need:
*   • A handkerchief*

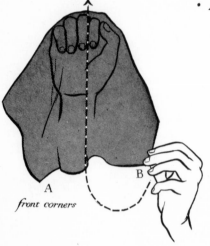

A
front corners
B

Here's how:

Make a loose and wiggly fist with the fingers of your fist facing front, away from you. Drape a handkerchief over the entire fist. Now, with the other hand, grasp one of the corners of the handkerchief hanging in front of your fist, (corner "B" in the diagram) and pull that

corner up between the pointer finger and the middle finger of your fist. Hold the corner in place with those fingers as you do the same thing with the other corner hanging in front of the fist (corner "A" in the diagram). Bring it up and hold it in place between the middle and

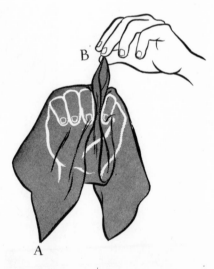

the ring finger of your fist. Your bunny now has two perfect ears and you can complete him by wrapping the remaining two corners of the handkerchief around your wrists as firmly as you can. There.

Now by gently moving your fingers inside the handkerchief, you can make your bunny wiggle his nose and flap his ears. Perhaps he'll even eat a carrot. He can do all sorts of tricks. I'm sure you'll agree that this rabbit learns very rabbitly.

HANDsome Johnny

Handsome Johnny is a famous television star. Have you seen him? For this puppet you will need:

> • *Nothing but a few crayons, and your hands. Isn't that handy?*

Here's how:

Draw in crayon or ink, finger paints, or lipstick, a face on the back of your hand. Follow the diagram for the position of the mouth. Carefully color the lower half of your pointer-finger and the upper half of your thumb. But don't copy the features in the diagram. Draw any silly face that occurs to you. Now make a fist, wrapping the end of your pointer finger around the last joint of your thumb, so that your thumb becomes the lower lip and your pointer finger becomes the upper lip. And that's all. As you move your thumb up and down, your puppet will talk, chew gum or eat and sing.

Try sticking the thumb of your other hand through the mouth. Whoops! Looks like he stuck his tongue out at you, doesn't it? Tsk, tsk, tsk. Mustn't let this puppet get out of hand.

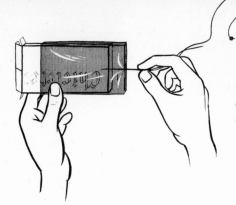

Your Gum-Chum

Be the first in your neighborhood to own a gum-chewing fish. For this puppet you will need:

- *An empty cellophane-wrapped chewing-gum box*
- *A needle*
- *Some thread*

Here's how:

Empty a box of Chiclets, for instance, or any other cellophane-wrapped box of gum, and push the transparent wrapping half off the box. Since you only pushed it half off, the other half is still on the box. Now grab the box, as shown in the diagram, holding both cellophane and box firmly in place. Thread a needle, knot the thread with a big fat knot, and insert the needle into the end of the cellophane and then through the end of the box itself. Push the needle and thread all the way through till the needle comes out the open end of the box and the knot is resting against the cellophane at the other end. You will find that pulling gently on the string will cause the knot to press the center of the cellophane wrapping in towards the box, forming a funny fish mouth.

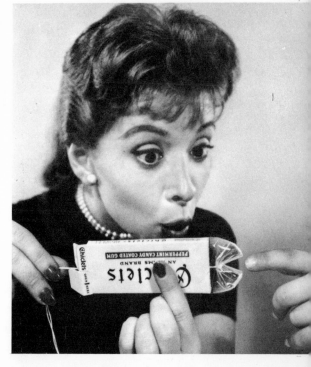

As you pull and release the pressure on your string, the fish will open and close his silly mouth. He'll nibble on noses and things that are offered to him, and if you care to give him a voice, he'll talk and talk and talk. Here's one fish that'll never clam up on you!

11

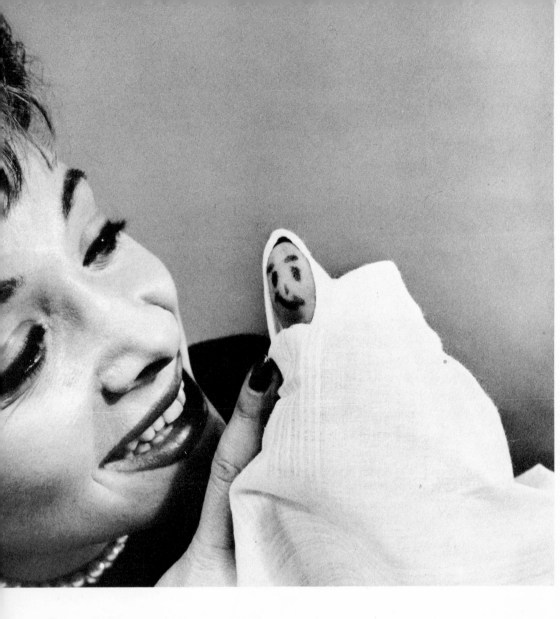

Thumbelina

Thumbelina is nothing more than a tiny face drawn on your thumb.
For this puppet you will need:
- *One thumb (preferably yours)*
- *A handkerchief*
- *A crayon or ball point pen*

Here's how:

Draw a funny face on your thumb and dress her up in a big handker-chief by covering her head, (be careful, not her face now) and draping the handkerchief under her chin. You can vary this by drawing silly faces on peanut shells or thimbles and then putting them on your finger.

These little fellows make good friends because when you want them, they're always right at your finger tips.

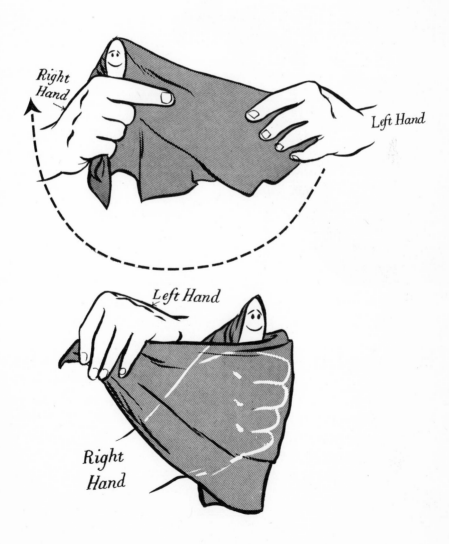

Chicky Mickey

Chicky Mickey is a cute balloon chicken puppet who lays eggs (balloon eggs, of course). For this puppet you will need:

- *A round yellow balloon*
- *Construction paper*
- *A pair of scissors*
- *Rubber cement or double-faced tape*

Here's how:

Cut (out of colored construction paper) all the pieces you see in the diagrams on the next page. (Of course, make your chicken parts to fit your balloon.)

Blow up your balloon (not too fat, please) and fasten the folded beak right over the knot, with the rubber cement or double-faced tape. Attach the wings, comb and eyes to the balloon chicken in the very same way. Make catstairs (they're easy—see page 51) and glue the feet (or claws if you wish) to the bottom of the catstairs. If you make a hole in the comb, tie a long string through the comb, and bounce your chicken at the end of the string, he'll dance for you.

Don't forget to blow up a tiny white balloon to be Chicky Mickey's egg.

Isn't he a slick chick?

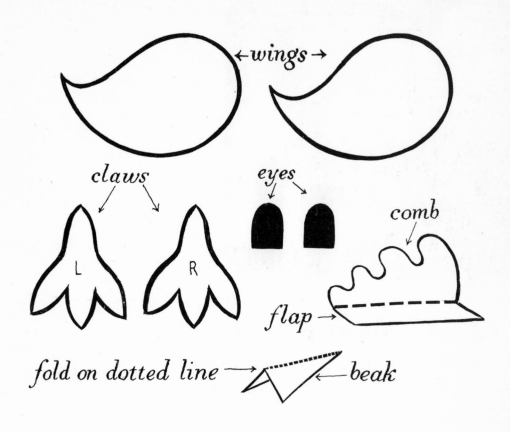

←wings→

claws

eyes

comb

L   R

flap→

fold on dotted line → ←beak

15

Apple Jack 'n Jill

This cute fruit puppet will be the apple of your eye. For each one you will need:

- *One round bright-red apple*
- *A needle*
- *A spoon*
- *A handkerchief*
- *A rubber band*

Here's how:

Sketch big pumpkin-like features on the apples, using the needle to break the skin as you draw. With a teaspoon, carefully scoop out the features that you have outlined. The white pulp of the apple will then show through the eyes, nose and mouth. This will shine brightly against the red skin of the apple face.

Have mother core the apple. Place a large handkerchief over your pointer finger, and place your finger into the apple core hole. After you have done this, put a rubber band around your outstretched thumb and middle finger. These two fingers will then become your Apple Jack's hands.

Your apple man can also serve as a candle holder if, instead of coring the apple, you make a tiny hole in the top of the apple and insert a little birthday candle well in his head.

But either way, doesn't he look good enough to eat?

Ella Fant, the Pachyderm Puppet

*Ask mother to help you make this cute fruit puppet. The next time she
goes shopping tell her please to pick out two turnips shaped like ele-
phants' heads: that is, shaped like round balls with long curved noses.
For this puppet you will need:*

- *Two turnips or squash*
- *A knife*
- *Two thumbtacks*
- *Two toothpicks*
- *Holes*
- *One other toothpick broken in half*

Here's how:

When you have these things assembled on the kitchen table, ask
mother to cut two ears (see diagram) from one of the turnips. (One ear
cut from each side of the same turnip.) Now the rest of that turnip can
be used for cooking. The other turnip will be the elephant. Have a deep
V-shaped slice cut into the turnip at the base of the long curved part
(which of course will be the trunk). This V-shaped slice is the mouth.

At the base of the vegetable (see picture for exact spot), have a deep
hole cut, wide enough for your pointer finger to slide right in. With

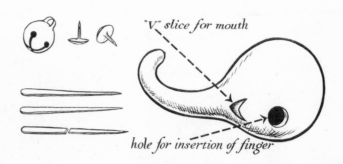

"V" slice for mouth

hole for insertion of finger

the broken pieces of toothpick, fasten the large round ears onto the sides of Ella Fant's head. Push in the two thumb tacks as eyes, and two whole toothpicks make perfect tusks on the sides of the trunk. For the finishing touch you might fasten a jingle bell to the top of the trunk with another toothpick. Now make a drape body, (see page 48 for easy instructions) and when completed insert your pointer finger into the hole in the bottom of the turnip. Lo and behold, a turnip elephant will turn up on the end of your finger.

Now that you've got an elephant on your hands why not let him star in your next puppet play? A circus show would be nice, or how about the story of Noah's Ark? You needn't worry about remembering his lines. They say an elephant never forgets!

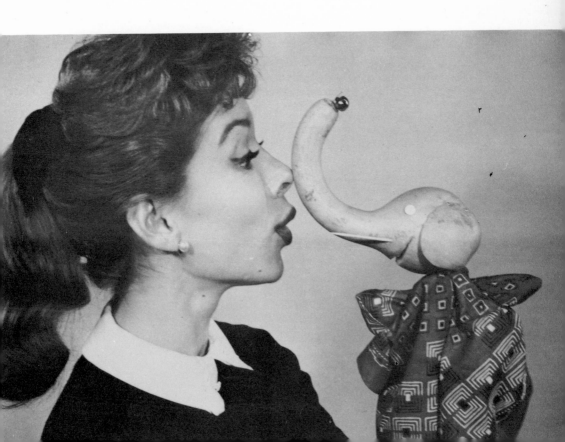

Winky

Winky is a handy little friend to have around. For this puppet you will need:

- *Your hand (as clean as possible)*
- *A ball point pen (or eyebrow pencil)*

Here's how:

Draw a face in the palm of your hand. Make sure that one eye straddles the fold in your palm directly under your pinky. Hold your hand up next to your face and curl your fingers down halfway (see picture). Now press down just your pinky and quickly straighten it back to starting position (bottom picture) and see how Winky will wink and flirt with you. Why not, you've got him right in the palm of your hand.

Octopussy Cat

This Octopussy Cat is as cute as a kitten and will decorate your room beautifully. For this puppet you will need:

- One hank of wool
- Ribbon (about 3 yards)
- Piece of string
- Soft rubber ball
- Pipe cleaners
- Pins or needle and thread

(CONTINUED)

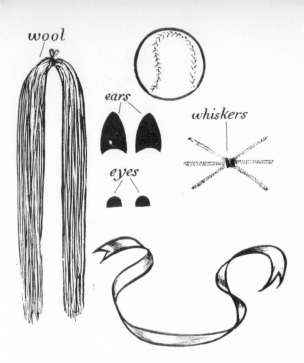

wool

ears

whiskers

eyes

Here's how:

Start with a hank of wool. Tie a string around one end of the circular hank of wool and cut the other end. Place a ball (a soft rubber one the size of a baseball would be wonderful) under the knot at the top of the hank of wool. Pull the wool around the ball, until you can't see the ball itself anymore, just the shape. Tie a ribbon under the ball to form the neck. Now cut ears and eyes out of felt, and sew, pin or paste them in the appropriate spots. Make a set of pipe cleaner whiskers, (see page 47 for instructions) and pin or sew them on in the center of the face. Now your pussycat is all head and tail. To change him into a full-

fledged Octopussy Cat, separate the remaining strands of wool into 8 sections. Braid each section and tie with a bow to match the ribbon at the neck.

Your Octopussy Cat is finished so step right up and shake hands and hands and hands and hands and . . .

Captain Carrot

If you carrot all for puppets you'll love this little carrot pirate. For this puppet you will need:

- *A fat carrot*
- *An old sock*
- *Three paper reinforcements*
- *One thumbtack*

- *A toothpick*
- *A pair of scissors*
- *A handkerchief*
- *A rubber band*

Here's how:

Cut off the toe of the sock for his hat. Just turn up a tiny brim and place it jauntily on top of the carrot. Cut another sliver of sock for his moustache. Stick the thumbtack through the widest spot in the center of the moustache and right into the carrot. (The thumbtack will become his nose.) Wet two paper reinforcements and attach them in the

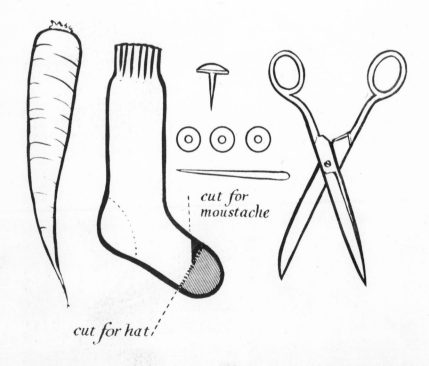

cut for moustache

cut for hat

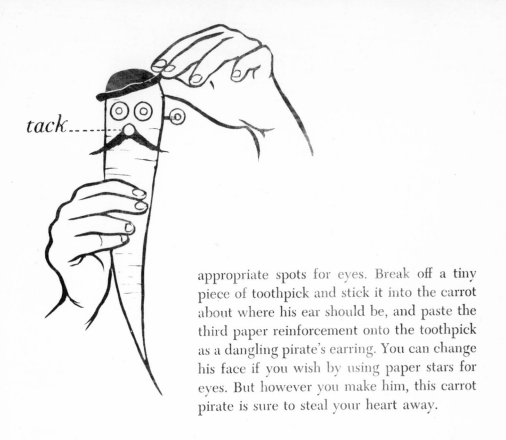

tack

appropriate spots for eyes. Break off a tiny piece of toothpick and stick it into the carrot about where his ear should be, and paste the third paper reinforcement onto the toothpick as a dangling pirate's earring. You can change his face if you wish by using paper stars for eyes. But however you make him, this carrot pirate is sure to steal your heart away.

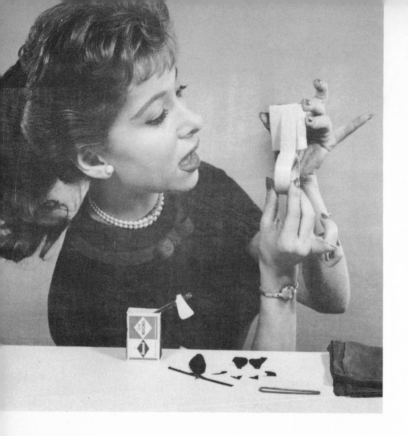

Willy B. Brave,

the Matchbox Indian

This matchbox Indian puppet, complete with headdress, will be a real feather in your cap. For this puppet you will need:

- *An empty matchbox*
- *A handkerchief*
- *A tiny feather*
- *Construction paper (or colored plastic tape)*
- *Scissors*
- *A rubber band*

Here's how:

Separate the two parts of an empty wooden matchbox, and throw away the inside drawer. Cover the outer shell of the box with red construction paper or colored plastic tape. Cut a thin band of dark paper (or tape) and attach a tiny feather to it. (If you don't have a real one, a paper one will do.) Paste this headdress near the open top of the matchbox. Now cut and paste dark eyes, a big nose, a snarly mouth and two huge ears to the covered match box. Use the drape body (page 48) for this puppet. The final touch is a pipe cleaner hatchet (paste on the tiny paper blade). This delightful puppet proves that fun is where you find it. Happy Hunting!

The
Funny
Bunny

This is really a funny bunny and so easy to make. For this puppet you will need:

- *A handkerchief*
- *A rubber band*

Here's how:

Hold the handkerchief by two adjacent corners as in the first picture. Place both corners in the same hand and grab the handkerchief (next picture) with the two corners sticking up above your fist. Now bring the bottom end of the handkerchief around the two ends, keeping them together as you make a knot in the very same spot where you were holding the handkerchief. You now have a knot which will form the Bunny's face and two ends sticking up above it, becoming his ears.

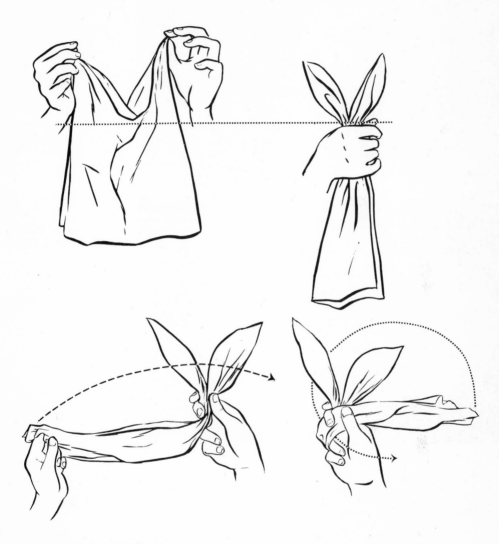

Shove your pointer finger deep into the knot and drape the rest of the handkerchief around your thumb and middle finger, which are extended in opposite directions. To complete the body, see page 48 for instructions on the drape body. Your pointer finger inside the knot will move the head, your thumb and middle finger will become hands. Here's a rabbit you can pull out of your pocket any old time.

Bouncer, the Ball Clown

This is the best known of all home-made puppets. For this puppet you will need:

- A hollow or soft rubber ball
- Some cotton
- A party horn
- An old glove
- Some crayons or paint
- A pair of scissors

Here's how:

In a rubber ball, cut a hole large enough for your pointer finger. Crayon or paint a face on the ball and rubber cement a neat frill of cotton around the finger hole. A party horn turned upside down is an

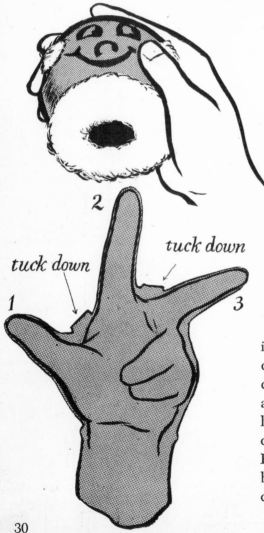

tuck down

tuck down

2

1

3

ideal clown hat, or you can make a cone out of paper, color it, and rubber cement it to the top of the ball. Make a glove body (see page 52) and add little buttons of cotton (also rubber cemented) to the palm of the glove. Place the ball clown head on the glove body, and your clown is ready to start clowning!

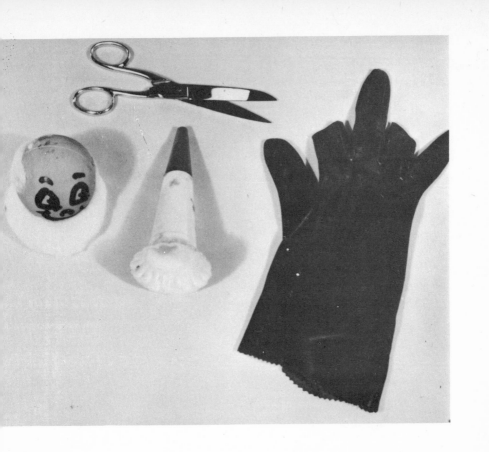

Coppelia, the Dancing Handkerchief

Here's a puppet's pal you can carry with you everywhere because for this puppet you will need only:
   • *A handkerchief*

Here's how:

Make a knot in a handkerchief at point A along the edge and right in between two adjacent corners. Now hold the handkerchief upside down so that the knot is hanging as in the second picture. Holding those two corners firmly, twirl the handkerchief away from you, around and around, over and over again until all that remains is a twirled rope of hanky, with two loose ends and a knot in the center. Grasp the two twirled ends of the hanky rope in one hand and hold your hands as shown in picture four.

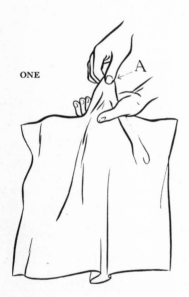

ONE

A

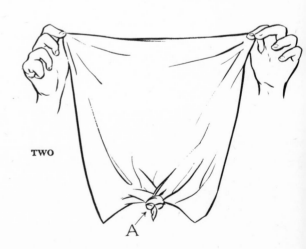

TWO

A

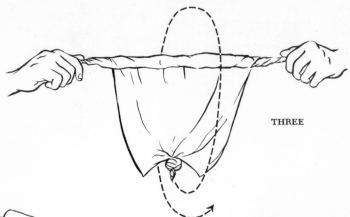

THREE

FOUR

If you bring your hands together and apart slightly, the ballet dancer will bend her knees and bow. To make her twirl and kick her legs high in the air, pull your hands rather sharply apart and let go of one leg. (But hold on to the other! ! !) Wheeeeeee! You can make her go through her whirling dance over and over again by retwirling the hanky as in picture three. After all, one good turn deserves another.

Sad Sack, the Bunny

The solution to your "what-to-do-on-a-rainy-day" problem, is in the bag. For this puppet you will need:

- *A brown paper shopping bag (the smallest you can find in the house)*
- *A pair of scissors*
- *Crayons*

Here's how:

Draw a colorful bunny on a closed brown paper bag so that the mouth is half on the bottom flap and half on the bag itself (see picture one). The top of his head should meet the fold at the top of the bag. Now turn the bag around and on the back of the bag draw the ears, so

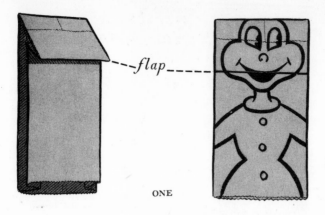

ONE

that they connect at the fold with the top of the
bunny's head (see picture two). Cut out the ears
along the outline except where they are joined
(at the fold) to the top of the head. Stand the ears
up straight and your bunny is complete, but

TWO

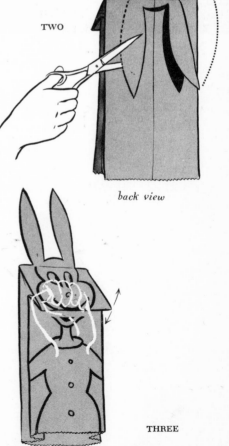

back view

speechless. Only *you* can make him talk.
Place your hand into the bag, so that
your fingers go inside the flap. By opening and closing your hand you can make
him open and close his mouth (picture
three). Next rainy day, the only sad sack
around your house will be Sad Sack, the
paper bag bunny.

THREE

35

Santa's the Name

(but he's just a shell of his former self)

Eggzamine this puppet. Only an eggspert could tell what it was made of. Can you guess? Eggzactly! For this puppet you will need:
- *A raw egg*
- *Some cotton*
- *Rubber cement*
- *Construction paper or felt*
- *A scissor*
- *A handkerchief*
- *A rubber band*

Here's how:

With a large needle, prick a hole in each end of an egg. Blow gently into the hole at one end and the egg will plop out of the shell through the hole at the other end. Enlarge just one of these holes gently, until your pointer finger can fit in. Apply rubber cement to the spot where you think Santa's beard should be, and then stick cotton right on to the

rubber cement, to form a big bushy beard. Do the same for the moustache, eyebrows and hair. A tiny paper or felt cone will become his nose, and two other tiny pieces, his eyes. Make a larger cone of the same material (either paper or felt) for a hat, and trim it with cotton. Then rubber cement the hat to the top of the egg. Now follow the instructions on page 48 and give Santa a drape body. Place Santa's head on top of the drape body and your puppet is ready to play. Isn't he eggciting?

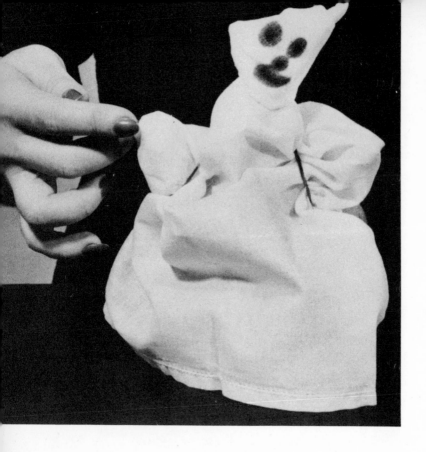

Boo Hoo, the Little Ghost

You haven't a ghost of a chance of scaring anyone with this little puppet, but a cuter spook cannot be imagined. For this puppet you will need:

- *A handkerchief*
- *A crayon*
- *A rubber band*

Here's how:

Knot one corner of the handkerchief and draw a face on the knot. Stick your pointer finger into the knot, and drape the rest of the handkerchief

around your outstretched thumb and middle finger. Hook a rubber band right around the thumb, across the back of your hand and around your

middle finger to complete the puppet body. Your pointer finger now controls his head and the other two fingers become his arms. See if you can make him scratch his head. He can applaud, bow, and rub his tummy, too! Why not let this enchanting ghost be the host of your next Halloween party? But don't wait until Halloween to get acquainted with Boo Hoo. He makes a spirited friend the year 'round!

Terry, the Washcloth Pussycat

Terry the pussycat will make a perfect gift, party favor, or surprise in a child's guest room. For this puppet you will need:

- *One square washcloth*
- *One cake of soap*
- *Three pipe cleaners*
- *Two sequins, or tiny buttons with straight pins stuck through the holes*
- *One half dozen other straight pins*
- *One strip of ribbon*
- *A pretty little bow (optional)*

Here's how:

Roll one entire edge of the cloth in until it reaches the center, then roll the other side till your cloth is a double roll like mine in picture one. Now pin one end of the double

ONE

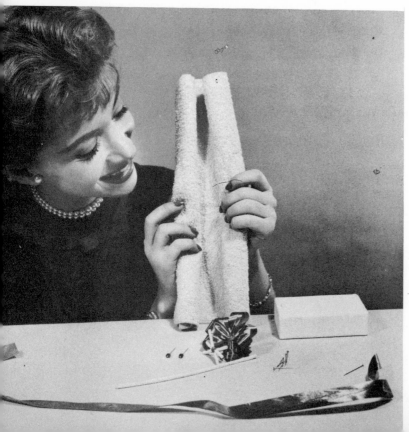

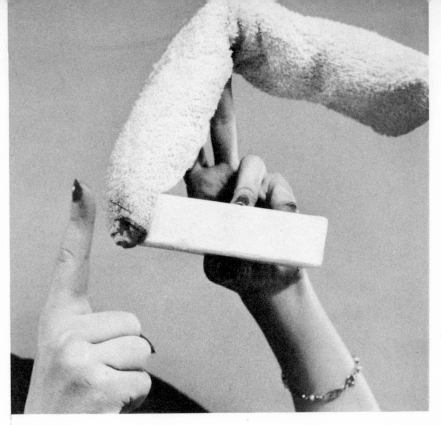

TWO

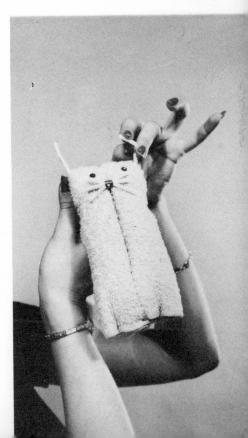

roll to one side of a cake of soap (as in picture two). Bend the roll in half and pin the other end to the other side of the soap. Make whiskers (see page 47 for instructions) and pin them on at about the center of the face. Pin on two sequins, or tiny buttons for eyes. Stick a pipe cleaner under the fold at the top center of the double roll of cloth and fold the pieces that protrude straight up and then in half to form perky little ears. For the tail, make a curl at one end of another pipe cleaner and then insert the straight end of

(CONTINUED)

that same pipe cleaner into the center opening in back. As a final touch, tie a tiny ribbon around the pussycat's neck and make a pretty bow, or pin on a little rosette, if you prefer.

Now, isn't he the cat's meow?

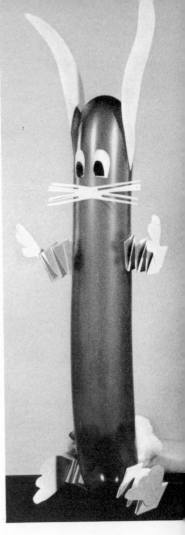

FIVE

For this hare-raising puppet, you will need:
- A long balloon
- Construction paper
- A pair of scissors
- Rubber cement

Hippity Hop

Here's how:

Cut ears, eyes, whiskers, hands and feet out of construction paper. Make catstairs (see page 51) for arms and legs. With dabs of rubber cement, paste the parts onto the balloon. The ears go on each side of the top of the balloon; the eyes go near the top, in the front; and the whiskers, below the eyes. The catstairs with hands attached go on each side of the balloon and the legs and feet at the bottom.

In back of Hippity Hop attach a ball of cotton for his cotton tail.

Tie a string around the knot on top and he'll do a jiggley dance for you.

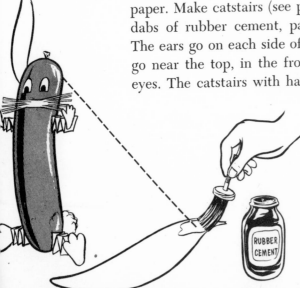

RUBBER CEMENT

43

Witch Hazel

Here's a bewitching witch for which you will need:
- *One salad spoon*
- *One party horn*
- *Some colored tape or construction paper*
- *Two paper reinforcements*
- *One cloth napkin or handkerchief*
- *One rubber band*

44

Here's how:

Hold the spoon with the hollow part facing you and the rounded part facing out. Stick the party horn right on top of the spoon to form the witch's hat. (If your horn has no fringe, stuff a few strands of wool or thin strips of paper under the horn so that your little witch will have straggly hair.) Now

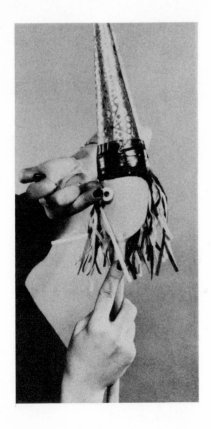

moisten the two paper reinforcements and stick them on the spoon to form big round eyes. If you wish, paste sequins or tiny circles of colored paper inside the reinforcement holes to make bright little eyeballs. Now cut from the tape or construction paper a long nose and a big mouth. My witch is a smiling sorceress, but yours can be the witch from Hansel and Gretel. Of course, she would then have a frown on her face.

(CONTINUED)

Make the body (see page 50 for instructions). For fun, try pushing up the stick from the bottom (with the other hand, of course), and just like magic her neck will grow as long as a giraffe's. If you pull, her long neck will disappear.

There! Now you know what a salad spoon witch looks like. What do you think a sand witch looks like? Hmmm?

Whiskers

Whiskers can be made of broom straws, opened bobby pins or thin strips of paper. But the nicest, most durable whiskers are these, made of pipe cleaners. For these whiskers you will need:
- *One pipe cleaner*
- *A strip of ribbon or wool*

Here's how:

Just cut a pipe cleaner into three equal pieces. Put all the pieces together, and tie them securely in the center with a tiny strip of ribbon or wool. Now holding them together in the middle, spread the ends apart.

You can attach the completed whiskers to your Octopussy Cat or Terry, the washcloth pussy with a straight pin or if you prefer, a single stitch.

Drape Puppet Body

This puppet body is as easy as 1-2-3: fingers, that is. For this puppet body you will need:
- *A large handkerchief*
- *A rubber band*

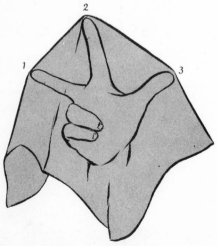

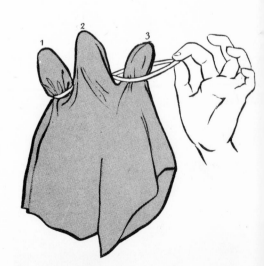

Here's how:

Hold your hand (the clean one) with the last two fingers folded onto the palm and the other three extended as in the picture. Now drape a handkerchief evenly over the extended fingers. Hook a rubber band over the handkerchief around finger number 1, pull it in back of your pointer finger (2) and hook it over the handkerchief and around your thumb (3). The head (a ball, or perhaps a fruit) is placed on your

pointer finger (2). The thumb and middle finger (1 and 3) become your new friend's hands—and there he is, right at your fingertip, ready to do your bidding.

Ella Fant, the elephant puppet with the squash head (see page 18) has a cotton handkerchief body like the one described above.

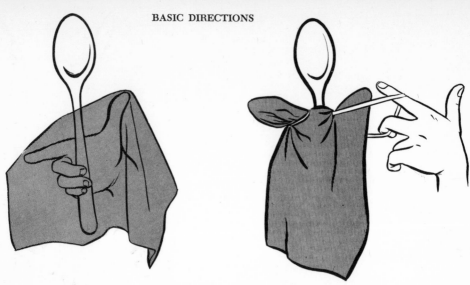

Drape-Around-Stick Body

If you want a puppet friend with real backbone, try one built around a stick of some sort. You can use a salad spoon as in the drawing, or a carrot, as in the picture. For this puppet you will need:
- *A stick (perhaps a spoon or a carrot)*
- *A rubber band*
- *A handkerchief*

Here's how:

Wrap the last three fingers of your right hand around the stick, with your pointer finger and thumb extending in opposite directions. Drape the handkerchief or cloth over the two extended fingers, and hook a rubber band around the pointer finger, then in back of the stick and last, around the thumb. Make a face on the part of the stick which extends above your hand and there he is—a little fellow that nobody will ever call spineless.

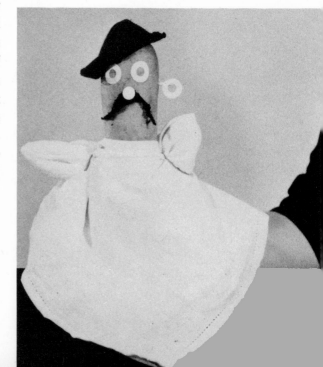

50

Catstairs

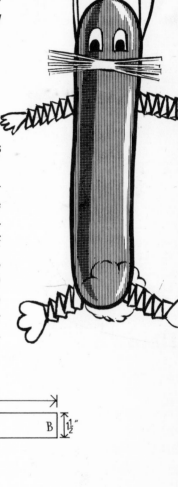

Accordian folded strips are called Catstairs. I don't know why, but everyone calls them that, so why shouldn't we? For Catstairs you will need:
- *Two strips of paper*
- *Rubber cement or double-faced tape*

Here's how:

Fasten the two strips together with their ends overlapping, as in the diagram.

Place your finger firmly on top of the two connected ends. With the other hand, bring one of the loose ends (end "A" in the diagram) over your finger and fold it down. Place your finger on top of the little center pile and (with the other hand, again) bring the loose end (end "B", this time) over your finger and fold it down. Continue to do this until both strips are entirely folded. Paste or tape the ends together. Hands and feet are attached to the end of the Catstairs.

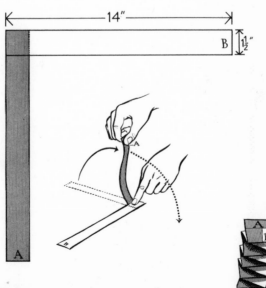

These Catstairs make wonderfully bouncy arms and legs for balloon rabbits and chickens.

Glove Body

Next time you lose one glove, keep the remaining one in your rainy-day box, for you will find that a glove body will complete your ball or fruit puppet very well indeed. For this puppet body you will need:

- *One old glove*
- *A pair of scissors*

Here's how:

Cut off the ring finger and the pointer finger of the glove, leaving just enough fabric to tuck in (for neatness sake). If you are working with a left glove, put it on your right hand, or vice versa. Hold your right hand, as in the diagram, with the last two fingers folded onto the palm. Now stick *your* right thumb into the thumb of the left glove, your right pointer finger into the middle finger of the left glove and your right middle finger into the pinky of the left glove.

Actually, if you'll just insert your right hand finger number 1 into the number one left glove finger, then your right number 2 finger into the number two left glove finger, etc., it will come out right. Your pointer finger (number 2) is the one that goes into the hole in your puppet head, and the thumb and middle finger become the arms. See how your puppet can bow, scratch his head, rub his tummy and applaud. He really comes to life for you!

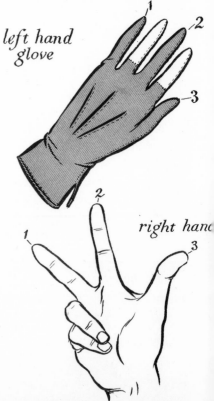

left hand glove

right hand

Apron Stage

This stage is most fun when three friends are playing together. For this puppet stage you will need:
  • *A big colorful apron*

Here's how:

The girl in the center ties an apron around her waist. Her two friends stand one on each side of her. The girl with the apron has two puppets, one on each hand. Her friends each have one puppet. They are wearing their puppets on the hand closest to the girl with the apron. At a given signal they reach down with their outside hands (that is the hand furthest away from the girl with the apron) and, grabbing the bottom corner of the apron that is closest to them, they lift it up way above their heads. The apron (if it's the right size) will cover the girl in the middle completely. She can lift up her two hands so that her puppets are dancing right above the bottom rim of the apron and the two apron holders can place the puppet on their inside hand behind the apron so that all four puppets can perform at the same time.

Cardboard Carton Stage

This puppet stage is a little more complicated than the others, but nevertheless easy enough for anyone to do. For this stage you will need:

- *A large carton*
- *Paints or crayons*
- *Scissors*
- *A bridge table*
- *A sheet or blanket*

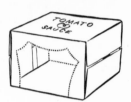

Here's how:

Select a large sturdy grocery carton and decide which side is going to be the front, and which the back. Remove the back of the carton entirely and cut the front so that you get the effect of a curtain drape (follow dotted lines in diagram). Next paint the entire box a bright color. Cover a bridge table with a sheet or blanket and place your cardboard carton stage on top of the table. Put the back edge of the carton right along the back edge of the table.

And now if you kneel behind the table, the blanket or sheet on the table will hide you, but the puppets on your hands can perform in the opening of the cardboard carton. If you want to change puppets in the middle of your play, hide the other puppets on the floor under the table and no one will see them because of the drape.

Puppet Tray Stage

This is a very unusual stage and easy to make. For this stage you will need:

- *The shallow top cover of a cardboard box*
- *A pair of scissors*
- *Some paint*
- *Some ribbon or heavy string*

Here's how:

Cut two holes, large enough for your hand to fit through, in the top of the box. Paint the entire box top a gay color.

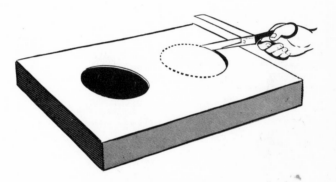

Attach a long piece of ribbon or string to each of the four corners of the box top and tie the four loose ends around your neck. Now put your hands up through the holes, put the puppets on your hands, and let them play, right there, on top of their own tiny stage. You can carry this stage with you wherever you go.

Doorway Stage

If mother will lend you a sheet or blanket you can make a doorway stage. For this stage you will need:
- *A sheet or blanket*

Here's how:

Attach your sheet or blanket across an open doorway at a point about one inch above your head. You will find that when you stretch your arms up your hands will show over the sheet or blanket, but you will be completely hidden. Place two of your favorite puppets on your hands and let them peek out above the sheet, and sing and dance along the top rim. It might be fun at a party to let the other children take turns having their puppets lead the group in community singing and games of "Follow the Leader."

101 Ways to Have Fun
with Puppets

Some of my best friends are puppets. . . .

Any doll-like toy that moves or "animates" is accurately called a puppet. A string puppet is called a marionette, while a hand-puppet is one in which your hand is inside the figure. (Generally, your pointer finger goes into the neck or head, while your thumb becomes one arm and your middle finger, the other.)

I like hand puppets best, because they come to life with so little effort. Is your little puppet puzzled about something? Rub your thumb against the side of your pointer finger and see him scratch his head. Is your puppet happy? Simply bring your thumb and middle finger together, and I'll bet he'll clap his hands!

You'll discover so many lively, funny things for your puppet to do. There are no rules. I would suggest that you try not to jiggle your character—fewer, broader gestures will be less confusing. When you have more than one puppet on stage at a time—it's advisable that you move only the one which is supposed to be talking.

Sit in front of a mirror for a few minutes, with your puppet on your hand and watch him—he'll show you how best to make him move.

Rainy-Day Box

The hardest part of any play project is the assembling of materials. Why not start a "Rainy-Day Box": a scrap box full of this and that, bits and pieces; things you have hidden away, instead of thrown away. Then on that "Nothing-to-do-day" that rolls 'round every so often, you'll be fully prepared.

Here's a list of odds 'n ends that will come in handy in making simple puppets:

Torn gloves and mittens
Old socks
Balls that have lost their bounce
Discarded jewelry
Old nice magazine pictures
Old hats (all kinds)
Construction paper
Scissors
Big, clean, but frayed handkerchiefs
Balloons
Scraps of materials and bits of fur
Brown wrapping paper
Old pocket books
String
Cellophane
Paper doilies
Crayons
Tiny buttons
Empty gift boxes and lids for stages
Thumb tacks
Feathers
Glue and rubber cement
Scotch tape
Pipe cleaners
Clean paper bags, of all sizes
Pieces of old lace
Colored gift wrapping paper
Leftover strands of wool
Crepe paper
Cotton batting
Rubber bands
Party horns and hats

Fiddle the Riddle

It might be fun to have a special puppet character who could be a riddle master. (I have found that most boys and girls enjoy the challenge of a good riddle.)

Your riddle master could try to stump your family or friends with riddles like these:

Why does an Indian wear a feather head dress?
　　—To keep his wig wam.
Which is the strongest day of the week?
　　—Sunday. The rest are weak days.
What is it that a cat has that no other animal has?
　　—Kittens.
What is yours and used by others more than yourself?
　　—Your name.
What fish's eyes are nearest together?
　　—The smallest fish.

Storytime

Stories supply richly exciting puppet material. The most basic stories (those known by all children, everywhere) can simply be improvised. Each child, having made or been given the appropriate puppet character, contributes to the dramatic action as *he* remembers it. Stories in this category include:

THREE LITTLE PIGS

GOLDILOCKS

LITTLE RED RIDING HOOD

THE LITTLE RED HEN

THE GINGERBREAD BOY, etc. . . .

Many of the well known Bible stories (e.g., MOSES IN BULLRUSHES, JOSEPH AND HIS BROTHERS, DAVID AND GOLIATH, NOAH AND THE ARK) lend themselves to this treatment.

There are so many *more* enticing tales, though, that it would seem a pity to limit your puppet plays to those you know. Why not have someone narrate a new story, as you, with the appropriate puppets, act it out in pantomime?

Try these. They're wonderful!

FOR HALLOWEEN Witch tales like "The Salad" (Grimm), or "Rapunzel"

FOR THANKSGIVING Feast tales like "Three Wishes" or "Why the Sea Is Salt"

FOR CHRISTMAS Happy generous tales like "The Shoemaker and the Elves"

FOR EASTER Bunny tails (oops—I mean tales) like "The Whiskers of Ho Ho (Littlefield)

FOR ST. PATRICK'S DAY Folk tales like "Little Dermot and the Thirsty Stones"

FOR APRIL FOOL'S DAY Puckish tales like "The Merry Pranks of Tyll Eulenspiegel"

FOR ANY WONDERFUL DAY Curious tales like "The Just So Stories" (Kipling)

All of these stories can be found in the library, and make good reading whether you *"play"* them or not.

Don't try to write a *script*, or *learn* your *part*—just pick a story you love, and everyone else will love it too!

Sing Along

It's amazing how well puppets sing, considering what they're made of. . . .

Some songs are fun to act out with puppets ("Ten Li'l Indians" and "Old MacDonald" lend themselves beautifully to this kind of dramatization). Other song games are nice to *play* with puppets: "The Farmer in the Dell," "She'll Be Comin' Round the Mountain" and "Here We Go Round the Mulberry Bush," to name a few.

Try three puppets, leading three groups of children in rounds. ("The King of France" and "Three Blind Mice," for example—but not at the same time, please!)

Puppets, I have found, play musical instruments very well indeed. (As well as you can play them—I'll bet!) They have particular skill with drums, tuned bells, xylophones, and other toy instruments they can handle with ease. Try it, and you'll see that you and your puppet can make beautiful music together.

I have found big fathers to be particularly susceptible to small puppets, and mothers to be very content with any activity that the family can enjoy together, so *do* make a funny little puppet for yourself— Your family and friends will take him to heart, and you'll find there's a place for *you* in the world of make-believe.

THE SHARI LEWIS
PUPPET BOOK